No Pianos, Pets or Foreigners!

My Life in Japan in the 80's.

JOE PALERMO

Copyright © 2020 Joe Palermo

All rights reserved.

ISBN: 979-8-6242-2611-1

CONTENTS

1	Prologue	1
2	Japanese Homestay and Love at First Sight	Pg 3
3	Japan Redux and the Pen Pals	Pg 8
4	The Perfect Interview	Pg 11
5	What's a Gunma?	Pg 14
6	The Dentist	Pg 21
7	Japanese G-Man	Pg 24
8	How to Become Japanese (or Not)	Pg 30
9	Life in the Office	Pg 37
10	Lunch with the Locals	Pg 40
11	Risking my Life and Being a Star	Pg 42
12	Facing Off with Primary School Students	Pg 46
13	Remember Your Passport (or How to Annoy Your Mother)	Pg 49
14	Buying a Car from a Catalog	Pg 52

15	The Great Cultural Divide	Pg 56
16	Experiences on the Wrong Side of the Law	Pg 60
17	Aiko and Shikishima Gakuen	Pg 64
18	No Pianos, Pets or Foreigners!	Pg 68
19	How to Get Married in Japan	Pg 75
20	My First "Real" Job	Pg 84
21	Meeting My Manga Hero	Pg 88
22	Life on Trains	Pg 92
23	Danger in Tokyo	Pg 95
24	Corporate Culture	Pg 99
25	Encounters with Suicide	Pg 103
26	Restaurants: A or B Set?	Pg 109
27	The Magic of Company Trips	Pg 119
28	Saying Goodbye	Pg 124
	About the Author	Pg 127

Joe Palermo

1 PROLOGUE

A young Japanese woman was running through Tokyo station screaming "Save me! Save me!" There was a Japanese man chasing her and closing in. He grabbed her wrist and caught her about 10 feet in front of me. The woman was still yelling "Save me! Save Me!" but the Japanese people in the crowded station ignored her, not wanting to get involved. Just another day in Japan. More on that later.

Sitting back in the seat of the 747 flight to Japan as a Mombusho English Fellow (currently the JET program) back in 1982, I thought about what one year of living in Japan might be like. I had visited Japan as a tourist on three previous occasions, but this was different. I had no idea how different. That one year turned into eight years, and some of the most interesting adventures of my life. I left as a newly graduated Liberal Arts (History) major, intending to teach English for one year and then return to a teaching job in the States. When I finally did return, it was as a businessman working for the A.C. Nielsen company in their newly formed Global Information Services department.

The stories told in this book are all based on my personal experiences in Japan during the 1980's in the places where I lived and worked. Please enjoy them in that context and don't assume this is representative of all of Japan. I have been back to Japan many times over the last 30 years. Some things have changed since the time I lived there, though many have not and are still deeply rooted in the culture.
Enjoy the ride!

2 JAPANESE HOMESTAY AND LOVE AT FIRST SIGHT

My first exposure to Japanese culture was through a course on Japanese History and Culture at a junior college in the Chicago area. The professor had been to Japan on 20+ occasions as part of his travels around the world. He was a popular professor and my personal favorite. I ended up taking several other courses from him. Through his influence, I changed my major to Teaching of History from Accounting (also, I was flunking accounting!). While studying under him, an opportunity came up to take a month-long tour of Asia in the summer of my sophomore year. He suggested this would be a better idea than just visiting Japan, in order to get a flavor of the entire region. Everyone on the tour was unknown to me, as it was not sponsored by our college, but I signed up anyway. The tour group was a mix of high school and college students. The tour included Japan (Tokyo, Kyoto, Nara), Hong Kong, Philippines, Thailand and ended in Hawaii. A separate book could be written just on that tour alone!

Japan was the first stop on the tour and the first experience would be a "homestay". Each person was assigned to a host family where we would live for one week and experience Japanese culture. My family was based in the city of Nara. The parents were two young school teachers who had two small children: a girl named Kumiko and a boy named Koki. The husband, Nobuo, was the only one who could speak English. At this point in my life, I had not yet begun studying Japanese, so we had to communicate in English. In Japan, whenever there is a homestay, it is considered polite if every waking moment is a planned activity. This differs greatly from the US model where privacy and free time are more valued and oftentimes Japanese students who have a homestay there would complain of being bored or not having enough to do, so that was a cultural learning right away.

Nara is in the Kansai area of Japan, near Kyoto and Osaka. The tour took place in August, so all of Asia was very hot and humid. The first night, the whole family was sitting in the living room and there were mosquitos everywhere. Nobuo plugged in a small heating unit about three inches square with a tablet on it containing insecticide. The mosquitos just started falling from the sky. That was an awesome sight and I made a mental note to buy one of those things before leaving the country!

Though many Japanese sleep on a futon on the floor, the first night at the homestay I was assigned to a bed in a room of my own. I happened to see a huge spider climbing up the wall near the bed. The wife came in and proceeded to smash it with her bare hand. At that point, I wasn't very keen on sleeping in this bed next to the "spider wall", so Nobuo suggested I sleep on their couch in the living room. That sounded like a good idea to me, so that's what I did. At about 2:00 am I started to hear sounds of something chewing on the wood paneling behind the couch where I was sleeping. I thought that was strange (creepy), but ignored it as best I could. The next morning, upon mentioning it to Nobuo he said "Oh, don't worry. That's just the mouse that lives in the wall." Great. While we were eating breakfast in the kitchen, I saw a mouse run across the kitchen floor and dive under the refrigerator. When I said "I just saw a mouse!", Nobuo replied, "Oh, he sometimes lives under the refrigerator." Oh, okay.

We went to visit many places during my stay. It so happened that the David Bowie album *Scary Monsters* was to be pre-released that week in Japan before anywhere else in the world. Since I'm a huge David Bowie fan, Nobuo took me to the local music store where I was able to buy it on cassette tape (1980). Those were the days when people still carried a Sony Walkman and could listen to tapes that way.

One of the places we visited was Nara Koen (Nara Deer Park) which is near Todaiji Temple, said to be the world's largest wooden building and houses the world's largest bronze Buddha statue. That's awesome, but something more amazing happened that day. One of the girls on the tour, Cathy, had a homestay in nearby Sakai, Osaka. Her Japanese host family just happened to take her to the same deer park as my family, and we ran into each other. There was a girl in her host family, Taeko, who was about the same age as we were. I spoke to Cathy for about five minutes and just said hello to Taeko when introduced. Little did I know that five years later, Taeko would become my wife! That's a story for another day.

After completing the month-long tour of Asia, I definitely fell in love with Japan above all of the other countries we visited. Upon returning to the states, I started my junior year at the University of Illinois at Chicago with a major of Teaching of History. As part of this Liberal Arts degree, it was necessary to study a language. Naturally, I picked Japanese and began to study it with a vengeance. Though I had studied Spanish in middle school and high school, it was not interesting to me. With Japanese, I had a goal to learn as much as possible so that I could visit Japan again and ultimately move there to experience the culture up close for at least one year.

3 JAPAN REDUX AND THE PEN PALS

The following year, I decided to go back to Japan and spend one month there during the summer. I had formed some friendships and had a number of "pen pals" who I was writing letters to on a regular basis. One of these friends was named Junko, and she and I shared a love for all things rock and roll, especially David Bowie. The first week of my summer trip was spent staying with Junko's family in Sayama, Saitama, which is just outside of Tokyo. I learned a lot about Japanese daily life from Junko's family. They took me sightseeing to many places, including the Imperial Palace in Tokyo. Junko and I continued to be good friends, even to this day. She and her friends were a big help to me when I eventually moved to Japan, introducing me to many places in Tokyo.

After my stay with Junko's family, it was time for me to fly to Osaka for the next leg of the journey. While we were walking through Haneda airport towards my gate, Junko wanted to visit the restroom, so I waited for her together with her parents. While we were standing there, I could hear a bunch of young girls screaming. I turned around and saw two members of the rock band "Cheap Trick" running for their lives through the airport, while being chased by a mob of young girls. I had heard they were performing in Japan and there they were! Junko's parents had no idea who they were. Once everyone ran by and it was quiet again, Junko emerged from the restroom. Knowing she was a huge fan, I ran up to her and excitedly relayed what had happened and how these screaming girls were chasing Cheap Trick through the airport. To this day, I still don't think she believes me.

Once I got to Osaka, I was to spend two weeks in a hotel near some other friends I had met, as well as a homestay with Taeko's family for a week. Taeko was the girl I had met the previous year at Nara Deer park. If you recall,

I had only spoken one word to her then. However, once I got back to the states, I was determined to locate my friend Cathy who had the homestay with Taeko's family, so I could get Taeko's address and write to her. The only problem was that I lived in the Chicago suburbs, and Cathy lived in California. There was no internet in those days, so it was not a simple matter. On top of that, Cathy's name was Cathy Brown. With "Brown" being one of the most common surnames there is, it was not going to be easy. I went to the local library and found the phone book for the area of California where Cathy lived. Needless to say, there were hundreds of entries for "Brown" and I didn't know her father's name. I did have one thing in my favor. I remembered that Cathy's family lived on "Lois Lane", the same name as superman's girlfriend! In the end, I found her telephone number and called her up to get Taeko's address. That was how Taeko and I began to communicate and get to know one another and I was able to spend a week with her family in Osaka.

Staying in Osaka is when I learned how different the Osaka dialect is from the standard Japanese dialect spoken in the Tokyo area. More about this later.

4 THE PERFECT INTERVIEW

Fast forwarding to my senior year and impending college graduation, I saw a job opening for a Mombusho English Fellow (currently the JET program). The job was sponsored by the Japanese Ministry of Education (Mombusho), which is similar to the US Department of Education. It included one year of living in Japan, as well as round trip airfare. There were interviews in New York, Chicago, and Los Angeles, with just 124 people to be chosen nationwide. I applied and was selected for an interview in Chicago, as I lived in the Chicago suburbs. The day before the interview, I decided to go to my local library to see what types of books were available on Japan. As I was looking at the books, I saw a book of essays by young Japanese primary school students on their impressions of the atomic bomb. What caught my eye was that the name of the editor of the book was the same name as the woman who would be interviewing me the next day. This was an amazing coincidence. I checked out the book and read through it that night.

The next day, I showed up for my interview and there were many students lining the hallway, waiting for their interviews, and looking nervous. Two people interviewed me: one was a man and the other was the woman whose name I had seen on the library book. They proceeded to ask me standard questions about why I wanted to go to Japan, etc. Though speaking Japanese was not a requirement for the job, I mentioned I was studying Japanese but did not yet have any fluency in the language. At the end of the interview, they asked me if I had any questions. I said yes, and directed my question to the woman. "Are you the same person that edited the book called "XXXXXXX"?" Her face lit up and the man next to her said, "You wrote a book?!" She turned to me and said, "You just won yourself a trip to Japan!" I walked out of the room with a big smile on my face with all of the nervous people in the hallway looking at me and thinking about what just happened in there with that guy. I'm sure there was some divine intervention happening there somehow.

5 WHAT'S A GUNMA?

Although I did get one of the positions, the scariest part of the experience was not having any input as to where in Japan the assignment was to be. I was assigned to a city called Numata, which is located in Gunma prefecture. Though I had never heard of this place before it turned out to be a beautiful city of 47,000 people known for farming and hot springs, all surrounded by mountains. It was located about a two-hour train ride from Tokyo, which made it popular for skiers in the winter looking for a weekend getaway.

The first week in Japan was "orientation", held in Tokyo, which all 124 of us attended, staying at the same hotel. We learned that some of us would be assigned to specific schools and others would be doing "one shots" which consisted of visiting a school and teaching three or four classes on any given day.

After orientation, my boss, Suzuki-sensei came to Tokyo to pick me up and take me to Numata. This was my first time meeting him and I was to stay in his home with his family for one week in a neighboring town called Minakami, while my house was being prepared. I was very nervous all week in Tokyo during orientation, as I didn't know what to expect in Numata and what my living conditions would be. I suddenly realized I was not just visiting Japan this time, I now lived there. I'll always be grateful to Suzuki-sensei for making me feel at home and cared for.

I learned that I would be living in a new prefabricated house that consisted of 3 small tatami matted rooms and a small kitchen. Japanese houses and apartments are laid out according to tatami mat sizes. The standard tatami mat size outside of Tokyo is actually bigger than those in Tokyo dwellings. My house consisted of two 6-mat rooms and a 4.5-mat room, besides the small kitchen.

Typical 6-mat tatami room

This house was small, but families of four were living in the same size houses on either side of me. To get to the house, I had to walk down a path which bordered a cemetery and a temple. The bath was a traditional Japanese bathtub with an attached gas heater that heats the water. If left too long, the water would actually boil. The tub was square but very deep so that when you sat down, the water level was up to your neck. There was a plastic "stir" that you could use to stir the water so the hot water was distributed evenly. The idea was to get washed outside of the tub while sitting on a small plastic stool on the tiled floor, which had a drain, and use the tub water for rinsing off. Then, once clean, you would soak in the tub, which was maintained at the same constant temperature using the attached heater. The toilet was a "western style" toilet in a tiny room of its own, but there was no water in it. There was a truck that came by once per week to vacuum out the underground tank the toilets flowed into.

I also had something in my house called a "hori-gotatsu". This is where a couple of the tatami are removed so there is a cutout in the floor which has an electric heater in the bottom. There was also a table with short wooden legs that fit over the opening so that you could sit on the tatami with your feet on the heater, like you were sitting at a table. There was a blanket over the table and then another hard-surfaced table on top of that. Therefore, you could sit normally with your feet on the heater while you were also covered with the blanket. This was fantastic in the winter! In the summer you could just turn off the heater and remove the blanket to continue using it as a table.

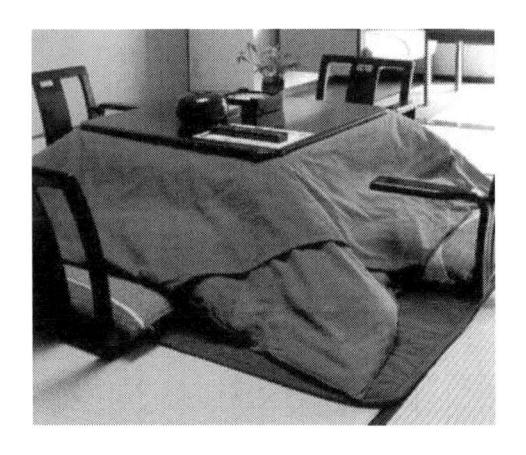

Since I am six feet tall, I had to duck through my own doorways, as they were so low. I hit my head many times! I also had to buy light fixtures, curtains, appliances, etc. The light fixtures just attached easily to existing electrical outlets for that purpose. Most of the appliances were purchased second hand. The education office where I was based, donated a desk and chair for the house. The owner of the house lived in town and I used to bring the rent money to his house each month in person so that we could drink tea and visit. It was very Japanese and very civilized. I also planted flowers around the perimeter of the house and got to meet the neighbors. The pressure for me was that most people in this town had never met an American before and I sometimes felt that whatever I did could be their impression of all Americans for the rest of their lives.

Although there was a space for it in a corner of my apartment, I never did purchase a washing machine. In Japan, the washing machine, by American standards, is relatively small and made of plastic. Originally they consisted of two cycles. First you had to wash the clothes and then there was a separate spin cycle compartment that was run separately. Eventually all of the machines were automatic, though only some were automatic machines in those days and they were much more expensive. All of the wash was done in cold water and the laundry was typically hung outside, unless you had a separate dryer which were all electric and took a long time to dry the clothes. I didn't want to buy a washing machine, as I wasn't sure how long I'd be in the country at that time, so I decided to send all of my laundry to the local dry cleaners. The only thing I washed myself were my socks, and that was done by hand.

The local dry cleaner was located about one block away and run by a very friendly older woman. It was a pleasure going there and talking with her, since she knew everything about the neighborhood. She would also hem my pants when needed and sew on buttons, etc. She really made me feel welcome and at home. I was into designer clothing and had quite a few Calvin Klein dress shirts that I had purchased in the US, which were quite expensive. I dropped them off at the cleaners along with all of my other clothing. When I went to pick up everything in a few days' time, I was very surprised to see that the lady had stitched my name in the inside collar of every shirt in Japanese katakana characters. She stitched "Jo". Now all of my shirts said "Calvin Klein" followed by "Jo" in stitching! I wasn't really mad about it, but was thinking how much time it took her to do this and wondered if she did that for every customer. I took my clothes there for two years and that was the beginning of a great friendship. I really loved the fact that all of the local merchants knew me and I felt they always had my best interests at heart and were looking out for the young American living in their midst.

6 THE DENTIST

In the US, people were obsessed with their teeth and it was not uncommon to go to the dentist twice per year for a teeth cleaning and checkup. In most other parts of the world, however, people only went to the dentist when they had a toothache or some other problem, and Japan was no exception. As a matter of fact, in the Japanese pop singer world, it was considered "cute" if the pop singer's teeth were a bit crooked or had a snaggletooth and were not perfect. I had always been brought up where I went to the dentist for regular cleanings and check-ups. At onc point before coming to Japan, it was necessary for me to have a root canal. This is where the nerve endings are removed from the tooth and it is replaced with a crown. In the US, our dentist was on the more expensive side. He replaced my lower crown tooth with a beautiful gold replica that looked and felt just like all of my other teeth, except that it was gold. It was a really nice piece of work and I was quite pleased and proud of it.

Having lived in my small town for just a few months, I decided to find a local dentist and go there for a teeth cleaning since that had always been my habit in the US. I found a local office that seemed reputable and made an appointment to have my teeth cleaned at a later date. The day finally came. The dentist seemed a bit surprised that anyone would come into his office when he or she didn't actually have a problem; he wasn't really sure why I was there. I explained to him that I just wanted to have my teeth cleaned. He proceeded to start the cleaning, attempting to use some pretty scary looking instruments. During the cleaning, he asked me if he could also clean my gold crown. I agreed, as I thought he would just polish my prized possession. Well, I was in for a shock. He proceeded to remove the crown and take it into another room. I don't know that much about dentistry, so I thought he would polish it and then put it back. No. He melted it down and created a new one. This new crown was completely oversized and consisted of a combination of gold mixed with other alloys. I was in shock, as the one I already had cost me a small fortune in the US, and was perfect. Thirty-plus years later, I still have that oversized crown in my mouth. My current dentist decided to just leave it and keep an eye on it over the years. Great.

7 JAPANESE G-MAN

As previously mentioned, I came to Japan as a Mombusho English Fellow. This is a fancy name for "English Teaching Consultant", which is a fancy name for "English Teacher". However, it was more than that. The job was sponsored by the Japanese Ministry of Education (Mombusho), which is similar to the US Department of Education. Therefore, I was working for the Japanese government. In 1981, 124 Americans were sent to Japan to expose middle school and high school students to "real" English conversation. Some of the MEF's, as we were called, were sent to work with a particular high school or middle school as teacher's aides. Others, such as myself, were selected to do "one shots". A "one shot" was where you visit a middle school and "teach" three or four of the classes on any given day. These were really just self-introductions in English, followed by a simple question and answer period. Later I introduced games that I created myself. One of the games was called the "Idol Game" and was based on knowledge of Japanese pop singers which were referred to as "idols". There would be questions about their songs, height, etc., in order to get the students interested. In general, English was required to be taught in Japan for six years. It was used as a way to separate the "men from the boys" on the high school and college entrance exams and was not taught as conversation. As a result, the average Japanese could read and write some English and probably understood the finer points of grammar better than the average American, but most could not speak it.

In Japan, everyone must conform and there were only two possible answers to a question: right or wrong. You will find that every middle school student in the country will be studying the same content, at the same time in order to get ready for the high school entrance exams. Japanese education is only compulsory through the third year of middle school, though about 97% go through to high school. The Japanese

Ministry of Education approves the textbooks to be used and the local boards of education choose from those.

I learned that I would be in the Tone Educational Office one day per week and my assignment for the rest of the days was to visit 50 middle schools once or twice within a year in the Tone and Agatsuma regions, and "teach" three or four classes in each one. The problem with this is that since most students were seeing me for the first time, I spent the whole year giving self-introductions and getting the students to try out their English, albeit in very creative ways. As I mentioned, there were only two ways to answer a question: the right way and the wrong way. Therefore, the correct textbook answer to "How are you?" was "Fine, and you?"

Well, on my first and subsequent school visits, when students would ask me "How are you?", I would say "I'm okay, how are you?" or some other variation. Their jaws would hit the floor when they heard a native English speaker give the "wrong" answer. This was their first lesson in real English. The important thing was to communicate, and not worry about the "right" answer all of the time. I've had students just clam up. Even though they understood the question, they could not simply answer "yes" or "no". They knew they must say "Yes, I do" or "Yes, I was", etc., and were so fearful that they would say the wrong thing, they just wouldn't say anything.

Actually, the most important thing was to speak English with the Japanese English teacher in front of their students, so that the students would realize that their teacher could speak "real" English and that this language was not just something to study, but was practical in the real world. Many teachers couldn't speak much more vocabulary than was in the middle school textbook, so this could also be a challenge.

The movie *E.T. The Extra-Terrestrial* had just been released. My favorite joke to the students was saying, "I am E.T." They would look at each other and wonder what I meant, since as far as they were concerned, I might as well have been from another planet! But I would follow this up with, "I am E.T. English Teacher." This always got big laughs. I guess I was practicing for my future dad jokes!

While visiting three or four classes in fifty

middle schools within a year, I met thousands of students. They all remembered me, as I was only one person. This meant that wherever I traveled in my free time, I was known by someone, but it was impossible to remember all of them. I did have a secret weapon though when I visited the classrooms. Out in these country schools, the students would change from their school uniforms into a type of track suit when they arrived at school. These track suits were color coded. The first-year students wore blue, the second-year students wore maroon and the third-year students wore green. Because of this I could always tell the year of the student. In addition, they had their names in large Chinese characters written across their chests. The beautiful part was they didn't think I was able to read these characters and thought I just had all of their names memorized. I would say "Honda-san, how are you?" The reaction was always "He remembered me!" That really helped a lot. Sadly, it did not help when I ran into these kids in their street clothes outside of school.

During the 1984 and 1988 Olympics, there was a speed skater named Akira Kuroiwa who competed. He won the bronze medal in 1988. He was from the town of Tsumagoi in Gunma.

One of the middle schools I visited was the one he attended. Believe it or not, almost all of the students at that school had the same last name of Kuroiwa. My favorite joke in class would be to shout out "Kuroiwa-san, raise your hand!" and 99% of the hands automatically went up.

8 HOW TO BECOME JAPANESE (OR NOT)

Anyone who has been to visit Japan for a week or two will tell you the same thing: "The country's beautiful, the people were beautiful and everything was so clean!". There was a lot of truth to these words, but of course, as with any country, this was an oversimplification and a result of not seeing all aspects of the country. Upon moving to Japan, however, I found that there are two ways that non-Japanese people dealt with living there. One was to surround themselves with Japanese people who speak English. In this way, they avoided having to deal with the language, other than memorizing a few words, for which the Japanese would praise them endlessly on their abilities. With this approach, however, it was always necessary to have someone interpret for you, and most Japanese tended to "filter" out anything bad to make your experience more enjoyable. There was nothing more frustrating than having a Japanese person pontificate for two whole minutes in response to one of your questions, and the interpreted response came back as "no". Really? Of course, they would explain, there is no word for "no" in Japanese, so people must express this in a roundabout way. I once knew a guy who lived in Japan for fifteen years and still could not converse in the language. The fact of the matter is, if you only surrounded yourself with Japanese people who could speak some English, all you really learned was how to speak rudimentary and strange English so you could be understood. When you returned back to the US, everyone you met would look at you strangely, as you spoke the simplified English you managed to learn.

The other approach was to become "more Japanese than the Japanese people". Fortunately, or unfortunately, as the case may be, this is the path which I chose. Having studied Japanese in college my junior and senior years, I set about poring over a textbook as a review. In addition to this, I refused to watch any television in English or to read any books in English. Any friends that I made did not have the ability to speak English nor had any interest in doing so. Lest you be wary, this was what was necessary to learn to speak Japanese fluently.

There were not very many Americans speaking Japanese back then, so any Japanese person I met could not get past my face and expected me to speak only English. They understood what was coming out of my mouth (since it was Japanese, after all), but looking at my face they initially assumed it was English and they had somehow developed the ability to understand it. Because of this, if I asked any question in Japanese, they would answer with every English word that they knew (which usually wasn't very many, especially living out in the country).

I had the experience of taking a young Japanese woman on a date to a local restaurant. When we walked in the door, a hush fell over the place as many people stopped eating and stared. Although I walked in first, the hostess directed all of her questions and answers over my shoulder to my date. The interesting part of this though, was that my date had not uttered one word. I was answering all of the questions, but the hostess refused to acknowledge that this could be possible and treated me as if I were invisible.

A friend of mine later gave me a very useful method to overcome this. He said, "it's very simple. Japanese people have an English/Japanese switch in their head. When they see a foreigner, a little light goes on that says "expect to hear English". At that point they are expecting English to come out of your mouth. If you speak in Japanese, they will just assume that it is English, whether it is or not. At that point, they will say that they don't understand English, or think that they suddenly understand English and try to answer with some form of English words. My friend's solution was effective. When you go up to a Japanese person to ask a question, he explained, say "excuse me" (sumimasen) in Japanese before you say anything else. At that point, the switch in their head will override their initial reaction to your foreign face, and they will expect the next words coming out of your mouth to be in Japanese. I have found this to work beautifully, especially with taxi drivers.

My purpose in doing this job was to learn

more about the Japanese culture, but also to improve my Japanese language so that I could speak, read and write it fluently. Little did I know that some of the townspeople had other ideas! I ended up living in Numata for two years. In my first year, I would walk everywhere. The walk to the local education office where I worked when not visiting individual schools was about twenty minutes from my small rental house. On the way there, people would actually lie in wait for me, as they knew the route I usually walked. I knew they weren't looking to harm me, as the crime rate in Japan is almost 0% compared to other countries, but they saw me as their "English Chance." These guys had spent six years of their lives learning English when they were in public school, and some had studied it in college, but they had never talked to a "real" native speaker before. They would jump out from somewhere and say things like "Would you like to drink coffee and eat steak?" I was very surprised by this and would usually put these guys politely off, since in my mind, my job was to speak English and my free time was to be spent in Japanese. Sometimes, in Japanese, I would say "Sorry, I only speak Spanish."

My boss, who was Japanese, gave me some very good advice. He cautioned me not to give out my name or address to any middle school English teachers. Friends of mine in other prefectures had done this and found that these people wanted to use them for their English at all hours of the day and night, calling for no reason and monopolizing their time. My philosophy was that if someone wanted to get to know me and learn about my culture, it made more sense to do so in Japanese. If they were willing to do this (we were in Japan, after all), then I knew that they liked me for me; and not because I was an "English Chance".

I made friends with the owner of a local noodle shop. It was a small shop with just a counter and about eight stools and I would eat there a couple of times per week. He introduced me to a friend of his that managed a local bar, as well as a local taxi driver he grew up with. The four of us would go to my friend's local bar once per week to drink and sing karaoke. Karaoke, literally meaning "empty orchestra" (Kara: Empty, Oke: Orchestra) was very popular in Japan in the early 80's. I used to sing in Japanese with my friends. I would purchase the cassette tapes and practice several songs at home. When we went out, I would act like these songs were randomly selected by me, even though I had been practicing them all week. Sometimes we went to a different, larger bar to sing. Whenever a Japanese person would sing, no one would really pay attention and when they were finished everyone would politely applaud with a light "golf clap", if you will. When I stood up to sing, you could hear a pin drop in the place as most had never seen a foreigner (gaijin) singing in Japanese, especially in their small town. Luckily, I can actually carry a tune!

The taxi driver's name was Tetsuo, whom we called Tettchan. His Japanese was really rough, full of slang and local dialect. I learned a lot from him! Whenever I was out with Japanese friends and didn't understand a word, I would pretend I understood and commit the word to memory. When I got home, I would write the words in a notebook along with the English translation. I had many notebooks that I used for studying vocabulary and spent many hours with them.

9 LIFE IN THE OFFICE

One day per week, or whenever I was not visiting schools, I was assigned to a desk at Tone Kyoiku Jimusho (Tone Educational District Office). My desk was right near the door, the lowliest position in the office. In any Japanese company, the new person always starts out with a desk near the door. Part of my job was to greet all of the people that came into the office during the course of the day. My "work" on these days consisted mostly of studying Japanese. The location of highest importance in any Japanese office is the space in the corner of the room, furthest from the door. In our case, this was reserved for the Tone Educational District Office Manager, whose desk faced all of the other workers. There were then section leaders who were seated at the end of two rows of desks pushed together. The workers in each of the rows faced each other, and the section leader was on the end overseeing everyone, with his back to the wall and window. Desk phones were shared

There were about 15 people in the office. Of these, three were young "Office Ladies" usually referred to as OL. Their job was to serve tea, wipe off all desks at the beginning of the day, and to do any other secretarial tasks that needed to be done. I learned a lot from these girls. They were the ones that gave me the lowdown on Japanese life outside the office. I also went together with them to see Japanese pop concerts and movies on the weekends quite often. This also helped me to understand the pop culture that my middle school students were interested in, and helped me to better understand them and use materials that they could relate to.

One weekend, I went to see a movie in Maebashi with Yukari, who was one of the office tea girls (OL). She lived with her parents within walking distance of my house. We planned to walk to the train station and take a train to Maebashi. Maebashi was a city larger than Numata with a population of over 135,000. When I arrived at her house, I was introduced to her parents. As she was getting ready, her father called from the other room, "Ask him if he wants some meat, we have some meat in the refrigerator." Apparently, stereotypes die hard, though I thought it was pretty funny.

10 LUNCH WITH THE LOCALS

One day, when I was home on a Saturday with nothing to do, I decided to walk into town and eat lunch at a local restaurant. This restaurant was in a typical Japanese style, where you could sit down at a low table situated on tatami mats. As was my usual habit, I brought along a Japanese comic (manga) to read so that people could see I understood Japanese. On this particular day, I was sitting at the table with my manga when I looked up to see the restaurant wait staff peeking around the corner and discussing who would have the unpleasant task of approaching the foreigner. They had nothing personal against foreigners, but in Japan there are social rules for most every situation and the worst thing that could ever happen to you is social embarrassment or losing face in public. Therefore, the biggest fear was that a foreigner would speak to you in English and you didn't know how to respond. Major embarrassment! Finally, it looked like the young waitress lost the battle and I saw her being gently shoved toward my table as the others continued to peek around the corner giggling and looking forward to watching the show. The young lady approached me and proceeded to hand me her order tablet and pencil without uttering a word. In Japanese, I asked her, "What should I do with this, did you want me to draw a picture or something?" The look on her face was priceless and she visibly relaxed as she realized I could speak the language. She took my order and then went back to report to the others. I heard one of them say "He's reading a manga!" The rest of them then came over to my table to talk to me and it turned out to be a fun time.

11 RISKING MY LIFE AND BEING A STAR

Visiting first-year middle school classrooms could sometimes be a dangerous thing. First-year students were usually the most enthusiastic and the most fun to teach. One time, I had been doing my standard "questions and answers" routine with a first-year class and one of my students asked me for my autograph. Japanese students write using characters and not cursive, so sometimes they would ask me to sign their English textbooks as a type of souvenir or memory. This was the final question of the class so thinking nothing of it, I made the mistake of saying "sure." Then I asked the student to bring his English text to the front so that I could sign it for him. A hush fell over the room as the students all made eye contact with one another. This could be their last chance for a signature! Then, all in one motion, the entire class jumped up from their seats and ran toward me. I barely had time to put my hands up to cover my head as the entire class mobbed me and tried to get an autograph. Finally, the teacher had to grab me by the arm and literally drag me from the classroom. I had never had anything like that happen to me then or since. From that day forward, I made sure each class knew they could get a signature if they wanted one before I left.

Speaking of my near "star" status, one of the schools had an annual talent show which consisted of all of their teachers performing on stage in the auditorium and showing off their individual talents or doing skits. The school principal contacted me ahead of time and asked me if I would like to participate as their guest, since I had visited this school before. The answer was definitely "Yes!"

I sometimes brought my guitar along on my school visits and sang a couple of songs I wrote to the students in between classes. I used to write pop songs in those days and had written about fifty in all. I had a TEAC four-track portable recording "studio" at home which I used to record my songs. I would play the guitar on one track and then go back and lay down the voice, followed by my own voice again singing harmony and then a drum track using an inexpensive drum machine that I had. For this occasion, I made my own "karaoke" tape, by just re-mixing two of my songs without the lead vocal. This then gave me the background music, as well as my own voice singing harmony.

I took my tape and had one of the teachers put it on for me as I went out on stage with a microphone in front of the entire school. The songs sounded great and the kids went wild! They started calling out my name and throwing paper streamers at the stage, just like at a local rock concert. Talk about having something go to your head; this was great! I only had a similar experience on this grand of a scale one other time during my career in Japan. That was when I was asked to play a song for another school's entire student body. That time, I played my guitar "live" and sang, but it was not nearly the frenzy I received at this school.

During this time in my life, I started to send demo tapes to recording companies in

California and New York, and though I received some kind words and encouragement, I never was able to sell any songs.

12 FACING OFF WITH PRIMARY SCHOOL STUDENTS

One of the things that visitors to Japan found endearing, soon became a major annoyance to me. That is the occasion when small primary school students see a foreign person and proceed to yell "Haro! Haro!" at him or her non-stop. This is cute when you are visiting Japan for a couple of weeks. When this happens every single day as you try to walk to the train station or to walk anywhere, it gets to be annoying. It's especially embarrassing if you are out on a date.

One day, I had a school visit that was only one train station stop over from mine. It was a ride of about 5-10 minutes. However, since the express trains did not stop at that small unmanned station, I had to wait for the local train that stops at every station, and this only came along once every hour. As I was standing alone on the platform in late afternoon, I saw the train approaching. Much to my dismay, I noticed that there were only a few cars on the train and they were filled with primary school students coming home from a local school trip. The windows were open and I could hear how noisy they were being from the excitement of the trip. I knew these students had rarely seen foreigners and I would be in for a chorus of "Haro! Haro!", etc. Since I did not want to wait another hour for the next train, I decided to board anyway. In Japan, the trains have benches along the sides of the train so that they can cram as many people standing up in the trains as possible. Therefore, most of the students were standing. When I got on the train, all talking, yelling, etc. suddenly stopped and you could hear a pin drop. I saw the young school teacher, probably about the same age as me sitting on the seat along the train wall. To break the ice, I made some comment to one of the students in Japanese, such as "How's it going?" Suddenly the student yelled out in Japanese, "He speaks!" and all of the students mobbed and gathered around me to shout questions in Japanese. "Who's your favorite singer? Can you use chopsticks? What country are you from?", etc. One kid asked me how old I was. When I told him I was twenty- three years old he said, "Hey, that's the same age as our teacher, why don't you marry her!" And then the students began to drag their red-faced teacher out of her seat and toward me as she apologized profusely. It was actually a very funny and fun experience. When I got off the train at the next stop, all of the students were hanging out the train windows waving and yelling "Bye, Bye!". Just another day in the country!

13 REMEMBER YOUR PASSPORT (OR HOW TO ANNOY YOUR MOTHER)

After living in Japan for about six months, I decided to go home to Chicago for Christmas. The plan was that my mother would come back to Japan with me after the holiday. I would take a week off of work and show her around Tokyo and Kyoto and after that she would stay at my house for an additional week while I went to work. Since I had to work during the day, she was pretty much on her own; although I did take her with me on one of my school visits. At that school, the teacher was much older and she was very honored that I would bring my mother with me on the visit. She was so respectful and kind to my mother that day.

When it was time for my mom to go back to the states, I had to get her to Narita airport. It was about a two-hour train ride to Tokyo from where I lived and then from there, we had to take a bus for another hour and a half to Narita. Since I was not leaving the country, I did not think to bring along my passport. Worse than that, as a non-Japanese citizen and permanent resident, I was required to carry around a foreign registration card (small booklet with name, photo, fingerprint, etc.) everywhere I went. I had forgotten to bring that as, again, I wasn't leaving the country. The bus had to go through a security checkpoint on the way to Narita. Police officers boarded the bus and asked everyone to produce their passports. I mentioned in Japanese that I didn't have mine since I lived in Japan and was just taking my mother to the airport. The officer then asked me for my foreign registration card. I told him I had forgotten it. He asked my mother and I to get off of the bus and also had her luggage removed (one very large suitcase) from where it was stored under the bus. We had to follow him carrying the suitcase (no wheels on them in those days) and walk to the police station nearby, which was quite a distance from the airport. At the station they were calling all of the officers over because they thought it was so amusing that I could speak Japanese. After asking me a myriad of questions, they produced a document that stated in Japanese that I forgot my foreign registration card through my own fault and stupidity and I promise to never do that again. Once I signed that and apologized, they asked me a few more questions and then let us go. I asked the officer when the next bus would arrive to take us to the airport. He laughed and said, "There is no bus. You have to walk. Don't forget your registration card again." We then had to walk about 30 minutes to the airport terminal while I lugged my mother's suitcase along. Needless to say, she was not happy with me and she almost missed her flight. Also, I got to hear about that story over and over again for the rest of my life. However, I never again forgot my foreign registration card! Lesson learned.

14 BUYING A CAR FROM A CATALOG

During my second year living in Japan I decided to buy a new car. This was mostly to avoid standing out when walking to the train station or around town in general when living out in the country. Up until then, I had taken a train to each of my school visits. Many times, the schools were so remote, the train stations were tiny and empty, with trains only coming once every hour or two, so having a car was helpful. It was also freezing in the winter. I would be the only MEF out of 124 to own a car.

Every day on my walk home from the office or the train station, I walked past a small Suzuki dealer near my house. This car dealership was just a garage attached to the owner's house where cars were sold and serviced. There were no actual cars for sale there and any purchased car would have to be ordered. A friend of mine had a small Suzuki car called a "Cervo" that I liked and I wanted to buy the same model, though hers was manual transmission and I wanted automatic. This car was called a "Kei" car, which means "light" as it had a very small 550cc engine. I decided to stop in on my way home from work one day and purchase a car. The owner's daughter was a middle school student in one of the local schools I visited (Numata Middle School). She was one of the girls I nicknamed "Wakame" after a popular cartoon character. I sat down with the owner, while his wife served us green tea, and proceeded to order a car from a brochure. Everything seemed to be optional, including the cigarette lighter, which was equivalent of an additional US $1.00. Ultimately, I had to have my boss sponsor me for the bank loan which was only to last six months. The car was brand new but not that expensive. I bought it in black with a red interior. It had automatic transmission, but let me tell you, trying to drive that car up mountains with only 550cc's of horsepower with the air-conditioning on was an adventure!

It turns out that when driving on the highway, there was one speed limit for "regular" cars and another posted for "Kei" cars. The normal speed limit was 100 km/hour (62 mph). For "Kei" cars, the speed limit was only 70 km/hour (43 mph). The first time I took the car on the highway I noticed a bell would ring whenever I went over 70 km/hour. Apparently, it's a mandatory law to have that bell in every "Kei" car, but it drove me crazy. I spent an hour looking under the hood trying to figure out how to disconnect the bell. Was it a fuse? What was it? As I was planning to take a ten hour drive to Osaka, I was on a mission to find out how to remove it. In the end, I realized I couldn't do this on my own. I went back to the dealership and talked to one of the mechanics, who seemed to be a pretty cool young guy. It turns out you have to remove the speedometer to disconnect the bell as that is where it is wired. The mechanic at the dealership disconnected it for me for free, but swore me to secrecy, since he was technically breaking the law. I'm hoping the statute of limitations is now up on that secret, as I'm telling it to you now! I did take that trip to Osaka, but I also discovered that once I hit about 90 km/hour (56 mph) the steering wheel in the car would start vibrating wildly. My only option was to hang on tight and turn the stereo up! I never thought of slowing down.

Once I bought the car, I decided that I would drive to my school visits instead of taking the train. Whenever I would take the train to a school, one of the middle school teachers would meet me at the train station and drive me the rest of the way. I decided that I would just drive to the train station instead and then I could follow the teacher's car back to the school. This worked out great, but took a great deal of convincing of my boss and the other members of my office, as they were ultimately responsible for my well-being. In the end, they supported me. My argument was that it was actually more dangerous riding with teachers in their cars while they tried to converse in English and drive at the same time!

15 THE GREAT CULTURAL DIVIDE

Because my spoken Japanese was now fluent, people would naturally assume that I also understood all of the nuances of Japanese culture. This was a constant learning curve as this can take an entire lifetime to understand, and sometimes never can be understood. There were different things I learned, pertaining to my social life, as well as life in corporate Japan. Many I learned the hard way.

My first cultural mistake involved my car and it occurred the first time I drove it to a school visit. Getting to the train station and following the teacher's car to the school went fine. The problem came when it was time for me to go home. I asked the teacher if I could follow him back to the main road and then I would know the way back home from there. He said that would be fine, so I proceeded to follow his car. When we got to the main road, he pulled his car over to the side of the road and got out of the car. Wanting to thank him for his help, I waved at him as I proceeded to drive home, as I might have done if I were in the US. I didn't learn until months (years?) later, what I had done wrong. It seems I was supposed to also pull off of the road, park behind his car, get out of my car and bow while thanking him for his help. I'm hoping he wasn't too insulted by my casual wave as I drove off into the distance and left him in the dust!

That was bad, but I can always remember worse instances. Once when I went to Japan on one of my trips in college, I was walking along the road with a female friend of mine when I saw a flower stand on the side of the road. Thinking I would be gallant, I offered to buy her a bouquet of flowers. She then proceeded to explain that those flowers were the ones people bought to put on graves in the cemetery. Okay. Romantic moment definitely over!

Cars in Japan are considered to be an extension of your house, so they are kept clean and new. There is a mandatory inspection after you have owned a new car for three years and then every two years after that. As vehicles get older, maintaining them to the required standards could become expensive and there was a cost for the inspection itself. Cars which can't pass inspection standards are not allowed on public roads. Unwanted vehicles must be exported or destroyed and recycled so you don't see rusty cars driving around in Japan.

Some people took their shoes off when driving, to keep the interior of their cars clean. I was pretty fanatical about my car, so I started doing that as well and I would also put tire wax on my vinyl floor mats to keep them shiny. One time, I drove my car to a supermarket that was on the outskirts of town so it had its own parking lot. Culturally, many Japanese shop every day and often walk to the local stores. On the day I drove to the supermarket, it was raining. When I came out of the store, I ran to my car and took off my shoes so that I wouldn't get my mats wet and drove home. The store was about a twenty minute drive from my house. Once I got home, I realized I had left my shoes in the middle of the supermarket parking lot in the pouring rain. Great.

There was a movie called *Back to the Future*, starring Michael J. Fox, that was released while I was living in Japan. This was the original, before the sequels. I had the opportunity to see that movie twice at the theater; once in Chicago and once in Tokyo. The difference in the audience reactions was a revelation in cultural differences. The audience definitely reacted differently while watching identical scenes. The most memorable was a scene back in time where a customer pulled his car into a gas station during the 1950's. As he pulled his car up to the pump, four gas station attendants sprang into action, simultaneously lifting up his hood to check the oil, clean his windshield, put air in the tires and pump the gas. In the US, everyone laughed at this scene as those days were long gone. This was a time where no attendant appeared at all and people were pumping their own gas. However, in Japan, no one laughed at this scene, as this is exactly what still happened there. Not only that, the attendant would also open up the car door and empty out the ashtray!

16 EXPERIENCES ON THE WRONG SIDE OF THE LAW

This wasn't a cultural difference, but more of me taking advantage of the fact that I was a foreigner. I decided to drive my car into town to visit a book store, and the only space left was a "no parking zone" in front of the store. I knew it was a no parking zone, as it had the letter P in a circle with a line drawn through it. In other words, it was the international sign for no parking. As I walked out of the store, there was a policeman standing in front of my car waiting for me. He said, "You're parked in a no parking zone." I looked at him and said, "Really? I'm sorry, I'm from the US and I didn't realize there was no parking here." To his credit, he just gave me a warning and said "Just because you don't know the laws doesn't mean you can disobey them." He was 100% right and I was wrong, and he said it with a straight face so we left it at that. Later on, that evening, I was sitting at the counter at my friend's small noodle shop telling him the story of how I pretended to not know I was parked in a no parking zone, when the policemen who gave me the warning walked in. Needless to say, I stopped in mid-story to greet him and thank him for letting me off with a warning. His only comment was, "Do you live around here?" Uh oh. We actually had a nice conversation and I really loved the fact that the local policemen often went door to door to meet the people on their "beat", asking them if they had any neighborhood issues and how they might help.

While living in Tokyo, I was on my way to a Japanese pop star concert (Akina Nakamori) in Gunma Prefecture where I used to live. It was a drive of about one hour and forty minutes from where I lived now. I was driving by myself and was meeting a friend of mine in Gunma who would attend the concert with me. Since the drive was so long, I was driving over the speed limit, but many other drivers were driving at the same speed. As we got further up the highway, there was a police checkpoint and policemen were flagging certain cars over to the side of the road. Unfortunately, I was driving one of those cars. It turned out there were speed cameras set up along the highway and we had been caught speeding. There was a makeshift table set up along the side of the highway with several policemen seated behind it and we all had to get out of our cars and line up to be processed. One by one we each received a speeding ticket. Very efficient! The interesting part of this story occurred a few days later. One of the police officers called me at my home. My license plate had recently changed since we moved from Saitama to Tokyo, and the police officer had written down the wrong license plate information when he pulled me over on the highway. Because of this, the policeman wanted me to come down to his station and present my paperwork. The police station was more than one hour away. Since it was so inconvenient, I told him that I'm sorry, but that was his error, so I'm not driving over one hour away to correct his mistake. At that point the officer didn't know what to do with this Japanese speaking foreigner. He covered the phone and I could hear him speaking to his supervisor. After a brief discussion, he got back on the phone and told me he was sorry for the inconvenience and that I didn't have to come in, and I could just tear up the ticket. That was awesome! I thanked him profusely. In Japan, the police are not used to people not doing what they say. Then again there is almost a zero crime-rate in Japan, so the system works. There are always policemen assigned to each neighborhood and they go door to door to introduce themselves and build relationships with the citizens in their area.

17 AIKO AND SHIKISHIMA GAKUEN

During the second year of my assignment, I learned of a girl named Aiko. She was a first-year middle school student, whose mother had abandoned her. She had been raised by her grandmother, but her grandmother was getting on in years and could no longer care for her. Because of this, she was to be placed into an orphanage. Being a member of the local board of education office, I learned of her situation and went to visit her home along with my boss. It turned out she was to be placed at "Shikishima Gakuen," which was an orphanage located in a village called "Komochi."

I promised her that I would visit her at the

orphanage. On my first visit to Shikishima Gakuen, I was struck by the oldness of the structure itself. It was all made of wood. There were many types of children there, some who were mentally challenged and had to be under constant supervision and some who were runaways or hard to manage children. One pleasant surprise was that many of the children at this orphanage were being mainstreamed into the local schools and some of them knew me already since I had visited their schools at one time or another. They were very excited to see me and I tried to visit the kids three or four times per month. I just spent time there playing catch with the kids or just talking to them outside. Many of the caregivers were volunteers and I sensed that they really cared about these kids. The principal of the orphanage was a very kind man. His house was within walking distance and his wife ran a day care center from their home for mothers who worked. He always welcomed me and encouraged me to come back whenever I wanted. On several occasions I brought Naoko, one of the girls from the office with me as well.

On one school visit, I saw that S-Chan, one of the young girls living at Shikishima Gakuen, was attending the school. She was mentally challenged and we had a nice conversation with the principal in his office, since S-chan knew me from my visits. That day, I was to visit her classroom to teach English. It was a first-year middle school class, so the students were quite young and full of energy. The first-year students were always a pleasure to teach, as they were excited about English conversation and weren't stressed out about passing the exams to enter high school, as the third-year students often were. There were some occasions where the third-year students felt my visits to expose them to English conversation were a "waste of time," as none of the material would be on their entrance exams.

I decided to do something to make the students feel like they were speaking real English and had a chance to interact with me. I asked all of the students to line up along the walls inside of the classroom. I told them I would come up to each one of them, shake their hand and say "How are you?" and they could reply with various responses I was teaching them. I started with the student nearest to me and proceeded to go from student to student, all around the room. Many students were embarrassed, but they were laughing and having a good time. Out of the corner of my eye I could see that S-Chan was about halfway down the line toward the middle of the room. As I got nearer to her, I could hear the students whispering amongst one another, concerned and wondering what would happen when I got to her, as she was slow of speech, even in Japanese. They didn't realize that I knew her already. I continued down the line and noticed the atmosphere getting tense as it neared her turn.

When I finally reached her, I shook her hand and exclaimed in an excited voice, "S-chan! How are you?," then in Japanese, "It's so good to see you again! I'm so glad you're in my class," and then I proceeded onto the next student as if it were perfectly natural. I could hear the other students exhaling collectively and whispering excitedly, "He knows her!" and wondering how that was possible. S-chan was over the moon and extremely happy with a broad smile on her face. I will never forget that day, and I bet she and the other students won't either.

18 NO PIANOS, PETS OR FOREIGNERS

Finding a place to live in Japan as a foreigner was no small task. When I first moved to Japan, the prefabricated house I originally moved into was secured for me by the local Japanese Education office, so the Japanese government became my guarantor with ultimate responsibility for my actions, though I was paying the monthly rent. I lived there for two years without any issues and I really loved it.

The rude awakening came for me when I was accepted to work for the Shimaden company in Tokyo and I had to find an apartment. The finance director at the company was assigned to take me around looking for an apartment or condominium to rent. In Japan, the condominium is called a "mansion" in Japanese, though it is anything but. We began looking in the prefecture just outside of Tokyo, which was called "Saitama". There was a running joke if you were from Saitama. The people in Tokyo would call it "The Saitama" and shorten it to the slang word "Da Sai", with the meaning being something that was not "cool". However, Saitama was a great place and we began looking for a "mansion" in various towns. In those days, the internet did not exist, so we had to rely on those hard copy apartment/mansion catalogs which featured listings, details and rent for all of the properties in the area. Shockingly to me, one of the prominent phrases in many (most) of the ads was "no pianos, pets, or foreigners". Many times, we would visit a realtor's office and as soon as I opened the door, one of the realtors would say in a loud voice, "Sorry, we don't handle foreigners!" In one instance, I was told they didn't handle foreigners, but they were willing to call other places to see if anyone else did. When the woman got the other realtor on the line, she covered the receiver and said "They want to know what country you're from." That was really the last straw for me that day, as I felt now the discrimination was going to be based on a person's country? Seriously? I walked out at that point. Actually, before I walked out, I said "Tell them I'm from deepest, darkest Africa!" Not my finest moment.

Finally, we were able to find a Japanese mansion that would take a chance on a foreigner. It was a unit with two 6-mat rooms and a kitchen with a wooden floor that was the equivalent of 9-mats, so you could actually put a kitchen table in there. This worked out well. The building also had an outdoor parking lot for a minimal additional fee. This was a different situation than my house in Numata, where I would pay the owner in person each month and therefore really got to know him. For this place, I was to have the money paid automatically by bank transfer, so I never was able to establish a relationship with the owner.

Initially, it was agreed that before I moved in, the owner would have the apartment cleaned, reverse the tatami-mats (this is a standard procedure when the mats became worn on one side), fix a small hole in the fusuma (a paper sliding door) as well as paint the walls in the kitchen. My taxi driver buddy, Tettchan, borrowed a truck from one of his friends and moved me and all of my stuff from my house in Numata to my new (to me) mansion in Sakado City, Saitama. The drive was about 1.5 hours in the direction of Tokyo. My new company was in Tokyo, but only about a fifty minute train ride from my new home.

When Tettchan and I arrived at my new place, I realized that it had not been cleaned and none of the other promises were kept either. I was not happy. After my buddy left, I began to clean the place and unpack as best as I could. That week I went out and bought some paint, varnish and other supplies. I then proceeded to spend the whole week varnishing the kitchen floor and painting the walls. I called the landlord and told her she would have to come to my place to collect the rent, as nothing she promised had been completed. When she finally arrived, she walked in and I noticed her looking around as if she didn't know what I was talking about. I explained to her how I spent the entire week painting the walls and varnishing the kitchen floor after it was promised to have been done before I moved into the place. She was very apologetic at that point and returned half of my rent for the month. She also had the hole in the fusuma repaired and the tatami reversed. That was great, because now that I had a place to live and a "real" job, I intended to ask my Japanese girlfriend (remember Taeko from my initial homestay that I met at the deer park?) to marry me and we would be living here if things went my way.

Another interesting house hunting episode happened after Taeko and I were married (spoiler alert!). After living in the Sakado mansion for three years, we decided to move to Tokyo, as I was about to start a new job there with the A.C. Nielsen Company. Even though she was Japanese, we were still running into the no pianos, no pets, no foreigners dilemma. We looked high and low for something we would be happy with. We finally found a mansion that was in a very large building with many individual units. I think we were looking at a unit on the ninth floor. The realtor was very kind and we loved the layout. The monthly rent was also quite reasonable. At that point, the realtor said that everything should be fine, but she would have to talk to the owner to see if having a foreigner live there was okay or not. She assured us it was just a formality, since Taeko was Japanese and I could speak Japanese and understood the culture, etc. At this point, I had lived in Japan for five years.

Well, it turned out it was not okay and the owner did not want to rent to a foreigner. The realtor was very apologetic and really felt bad. I suggested that I meet with the owner face to face and was sure that once he met me and realized I could speak Japanese fluently and had lived in Japan for five years already, he would be more than willing to rent to us. I tried not to take these situations too personally, as I was the one who chose to live in Japan and therefore, should follow the rules of that culture. The owner agreed to meet with me at the building. I started off by giving him the traditional bow and then talked about how I had worked for the Japanese government department of education and was now working for a Japanese company in Tokyo and I intended to live in Japan for many years. He let me finish my story, thanked me for my time and said he was very sorry, but he just could not rent the apartment to me. I asked him why not and his answer is one I will never forget. He said "It's not because you're a foreigner. It's just because you are not Japanese." Somehow this logic made sense to him and I realized at that moment there was no way I was going to change this guy's mind; it was time to move on.

This turned out to be a blessing in disguise. Instead of living in that giant building with one apartment on top of the other, our realtor found us a brand new mansion that was only four stories tall. The unit we fell in love with was a corner unit on the third floor and was right next to a beautiful Japanese temple with lots of green all around in a very quiet area. It was what they called a 2 LDK. LDK stands for living room, dining room and kitchen. It had two 6-mat rooms, one with tatami mats and one with carpeting. It also had a very large living dining area that was also carpeted and a small kitchen. Down the long hallway was the Japanese bath and toilet (with actual water in it!). It also had an intercom system on the ground floor so people had to be buzzed in for the entryway doors to open. It was almost twice the price of the mansion we had in Saitama, but we decided it was worth it. We had to rent a parking space a couple of blocks away for our car, but we couldn't be happier. The woman who was the landlord was very nice and she would come and visit with us a couple of times per year to see how we were doing.

19 HOW TO GET MARRIED IN JAPAN

Though Taeko and I had been dating for two years via a long distance romance (she in Osaka, and me in Numata), I vowed to not get married until I had a "real job". We were separated by quite a distance: two hours from Numata to Tokyo by train and then fifty minutes by plane or three hours by bullet train to Osaka. Taeko would write me letters every day in Japanese to help me with my reading. For a while, she would write in the Osaka dialect, as it was quite different from Tokyo and I wanted to learn it so that I could better understand what her relatives were saying, especially her grandparents who used the dialect heavily.

I initially wanted to find a job in Osaka, but I was made aware of a job at a company called Shimaden in Tokyo. This was a small traditional Japanese company run by two brothers. Their business was manufacturing and selling temperature controllers for industry and they competed against some larger Japanese powerhouses, such as Omron. They were advertising for a Japanese national who could speak English. I thought, why not a native English speaker who could speak and read Japanese?

There was a standard resume form sold in local stationary stores that everyone filled out. I decided to purchase and complete one of these and send it along to the company. A photo was also required as part of the resume, so they could see right away that I was not Japanese. The form was mailed and now it was time to wait.

To my surprise, I received a phone call from the Export Director to come in for an interview, as they were interested.

To make a long story short, I was hired for the position on the spot after the interview. The role was in their export department. It was just myself and the Export Director. We divided up multiple subsidiaries around the world and were responsible for answering all of their product questions, as well as placing their orders. I was also responsible for translating product instructions and sales brochures into English. I loved it as I spent a lot of time liaising with the Head of Operations and the Head of Engineering to get the answers for our subsidiaries as to what could or couldn't be done. This was a great experience, as I was the only non-Japanese person in the company.

Now that I had a "real job", I armed myself with the company brochures and prepared to fly to Osaka to ask Taeko's father's permission for her hand in marriage. Obviously, I had already gotten a "yes" from Taeko, but now I had to research the right words to use with her father. I put on my best suit (actually it was a light purple sport coat and tie) and made the long trip to Osaka.

Taeko lived with her family (3 generations), so I already knew her parents and grandparents well and had a brief homestay there in the past, as I mentioned. As soon as I arrived, I greeted everyone and began to tell her father about my new job and to show him the brochure and explain all of the benefits I would receive. It was important to me that we get his permission to be married as I wanted to be engaged to Taeko before taking her back to the US to meet my family and friends, though we would be living in Japan after marriage. We talked and talked, as I could not get up the nerve to ask him the crucial question. Eventually, it was getting late and everyone started leaving the room until it was just he and I left in the living room. Finally, he said he had to get to bed as he was getting up early to go golfing in the morning. That was my cue, so I popped the question. "Please give me Taeko's hand in marriage". Obviously, he knew why I was there and he let me sweat it out until that point. I told him I wanted to live in Japan indefinitely (as I did at that point) and I wanted Taeko to come with me to the US for a couple of weeks to meet my relatives. At the end of all of this, he told me he would give me his answer in the morning. He went to bed, and since I was staying at his house, so did I, wondering what the morning would bring.

The news the next day turned out to be better than I hoped. He left word with Taeko's mother that he approved and not only that, he would pay Taeko's airfare for our trip back to the US to meet my relatives. Outstanding!

We did end up traveling back to Chicago and had a great time while we were there. I had told Taeko that I couldn't afford a ring, but then I secretly purchased a diamond ring, surprising her with it on her birthday. My friend from the noodle shop had introduced me to a local jeweler he knew. When Taeko saw the ring, she cried. When I originally saw the price, I cried.

While we were in a large shopping mall in the US, I suggested we stop at the jewelry store to see what they thought the ring was worth. The conversation went something like this:

Me: "Hi. My wife and I will be getting married soon and I bought this ring for her in Japan. Can you tell me how much it would cost if I had purchased it here?". I told him the price I paid for the ring. The jeweler put in his eyepiece, took a close look at the diamond and asked: "Do you love her?" (I knew I was in trouble then).
Me: "Yes, of course I do".
Jeweler: "Never buy jewelry in Japan!"

Well, that was definitely a lesson learned and very true. For example, the prices in the

Tiffany & Co. mail order catalog or website in Japan were 3x the prices when purchasing in the US.

We decided we would be married in Japan and just have a ceremony but not any kind of reception. We knew if we had a reception, we would have to have one in Japan and also one in the US and we were just not prepared for that. Since we planned to live in Japan, we decided to get married at a local Presbyterian Church that Taeko's grandmother attended. It was extremely rare that Taeko and her grandmother were Christians, as less than 1% of the population in Japan claims Christian faith or affiliation, even to this day. The plan was to get married and then Taeko would join me in Sakado City, Saitama, where I had just moved. We would later spend 10 days in Kauai on our honeymoon.

We wanted to keep the cost of everything down, so we decided to rent my tuxedo and Taeko's wedding dress. After the wedding, my now in-laws took those in attendance out to dinner and presented them with small gifts we had purchased, according to tradition. Taeko and I headed off to a hotel in Osaka where we spent the night before flying back to Tokyo in the morning. A month later we took our honeymoon in Hawaii. We stayed at the Coco Palms Resort on the island of Kauai for eight days. This was the same place where Elvis Presley appeared in the film "*Blue Hawaii*", but it has since been destroyed by a hurricane.

In a traditional Japanese wedding, the bride and groom change clothes several times during the ceremony with the bride wearing a wedding dress, a kimono that matches the season and then a wedding kimono. Afterwards, at the reception there is lots of eating and drinking with people taking turns giving speeches. There is no music or dancing. We were to have a "western style" wedding, which means it would be celebrated as in the western culture, not a cowboy wedding, in case some of you were thinking that! Taeko's father walked her down the aisle in the church and then we said our vows in Japanese. I still remember standing at the altar and seeing Taeko for the first time as she walked down the aisle with her father. She was beautiful and I almost started bawling right then and there. There's no way I deserved her.

Since none of Taeko's relatives had ever been to a church wedding before, we had quite a few people show up for the ceremony. In addition, we had a professional photographer to take pictures before, during and after. I had rented a white tuxedo. The main controversy involved the white gloves that came with the tuxedo. I refused to wear them, but the photographer kept insisting over and over that I do, and complaining that no one had ever not worn them before. Until now, since there was no way I was wearing white gloves.

Well, the wedding went perfect and without a hitch. I really have no idea what I promised during the Japanese ceremony, but I hope that I have lived up to those promises! Depending on what day it is, Taeko will say that I did. As of this writing, we have been married for thirty-five years.

Fast forward to our first wedding anniversary. We decided to stay at the Century Hyatt Hotel (now Hyatt Regency) in Shinjuku, Tokyo for a night to celebrate. This was during the "disco" craze and I loved dancing and was really looking forward to it. After a fantastic dinner, we went into the "disco" there in the hotel to have a drink and to dance. There was a Japanese wedding party there that was getting a little rowdy on the dance floor. They were feeling their alcohol and were not good dancers to begin with. They stepped on our feet a couple of times, so we took a break. Still angry from having our dancing interrupted, I decided to head over to the men's room. It was one of those deals where only one person could be in there at a time.

I went in and locked the door. As I was doing my business, someone knocked on the door. In Japan, if you are in a restroom stall or any bathroom and someone knocks on the door and it is occupied, the protocol is that the occupant simply knocks back to show someone is in there already. I knocked back, but then this guy just starts pounding on the door. At that point I was annoyed so I yanked open the door and said in Japanese, "What's the big hurry" while staring with my "mean" face. The look on the guy's face was priceless, as he expected a Japanese person to be in there, not some American chewing him out in Japanese. After that we headed back out to the dance floor and managed to have a great time.

20 MY FIRST "REAL" JOB

My job at Shimaden actually started about a month or so before I was to get married. Believe it or not, after only being on the job for a couple of weeks, I was charged with accompanying the Managing Director (one of the owners) of the company on a multi-country trip across Asia, as his interpreter. We visited Taiwan, Hong Kong, Australia and New Zealand. The trip only lasted a week, so it was quite stressful. For example, the flight time from Tokyo to Australia is eight hours, so you can see there was a lot of flying time as well to visit four countries.

The first stop was Taiwan and I had always wanted to stay at the Grand Hotel in Taipei, as my college professor had stayed there and mentioned it was one of the best hotels he had ever stayed in. Since I was responsible for booking the whole trip, I made sure we got to stay there. The lobby was beautiful and magnificent and did not disappoint. However, the actual room had no windows. Wait, I take that back. There was one rectangular window with a curtain over it. Upon opening the curtain, I realized it was a window looking out into the hallway! I have stayed at hundreds of hotels over the years all over the world, and I have never seen anything like it since (I'm happy to say).

In each of the countries, we were to meet with the owner of the subsidiary where we had established a partnership. Taiwan was one of our more profitable subsidiaries and we met with Mr. Lee in the lobby of our hotel to begin the day. Though he was Chinese, he communicated in English, which I had to translate into Japanese. While we were meeting, I noticed a small red dot on my neck that was very itchy. I assumed this was some kind of spider bite or something and didn't pay it too much attention. The day in Taipei went well and we also had a wonderful dinner with Mr. Lee. It was now time for us to move on to Hong Kong. As we continued with our trip, I noticed that the small spot on my neck was continuing to spread to my chest. By the time we got to Australia, this rash had covered my entire body below my neck. I managed to call the hotel doctor and she was only able to give me a large tube of steroid cream that she suggested I spread all over my body. I'm pretty sure my body had broken out into hives due to the stress of visiting these countries for the first time (with the exception of Hong Kong, which I had visited before), interpreting for the owner of the company after only working there a few weeks, and the fact that I was to get married one week after our return!

Once we finally returned to Japan and I was able to visit a dermatologist, I realized these were hives probably caused by stress. He prescribed prednisone, which would remove the hives, but then I had to taper off from it. Though I looked fine on my wedding day, my body was actually covered in hives during the ceremony.

Shimaden bought a company car called the "Nissan President". It was a large four door model; the type used to chauffeur people around. It had a phone in the back seat arm rest, which was extremely rare for the time.

Whenever we had a visitor from one of our overseas subsidiaries, we would pick them up from the airport in the car and we would also use it to drive them to our factory in the Tokyo suburbs. On the way from the home office to the factory, our company president, riding in the back with the client, would always call ahead on the car phone to impress our visitor. The pretense was that he had to call ahead to make sure the factory was ready for our visit. Sometimes I would be the driver.

Once our subsidiary head from the US came to visit with his wife. Since I was responsible for the US business, I drove the car to Narita airport to pick them up. The president of our company was riding in the back. When we got to the airport checkpoint, which all cars must pass through, they were really surprised to see a twenty- something American driving a Japanese president around.

21 MEETING MY MANGA HERO

While living in Sakado and working at Shimaden, I decided to join a gym to get some exercise. This place was a gym and then had another section with pool tables (billiards), as playing pool was getting popular in Japan again, especially after the movie *The Color of Money* came out, which was a sequel to *The Hustler* and starred Paul Newman and Tom Cruise. Instead of working out in the gym on my own, I joined a "weight training class." This basically consisted of a trainer telling a group of us what to do, and we just did what he said. There were some crazy exercises. The workout always started with an intense run around the neighborhood as a warmup before we began. The first night I came home from the training, I was so exhausted that I couldn't eat and felt physically sick. In the class I met Yasuhiro Nakanishi, who drew and wrote Japanese comics (manga) for what is now the largest publishing company in Japan, called Kodansha. His comics were appearing in the weekly comic magazine called *Shonen Magazine*. These weekly comics were volumes about two inches thick that were printed on newsprint and featured multiple stories by various comic writers that continued each week. One of these called *Weekly Shonen Jump* produced by Shueisha, was actually in the *Guinness Book of World Records* as the largest selling weekly magazine in the world, outselling both *Time* and *Newsweek*. Comics were and are serious business in Japan. Each individual story within the weekly comic would also be published separately as a book in a numbered series. In the US, we call these trade paperbacks. Since I loved reading comics, I quickly became friends with "Nakanishi-sensei" ("Sensei" is a term bestowed on teachers, authors and other artists). He lived in a condo one town over from me and he rented another condo across the street from where he lived, to use as his office, since he would work at all hours of the night. Many comic writers used assistants to draw the comic backgrounds, lettering, etc., but Nakanishi-sensei would do everything himself. I really liked his drawing style.

Each year, every Japanese company has an end of the year party for their employees called a "bonenkai". Nakanishi-sensei invited my wife Taeko and I to the bonenkai at Kodansha, which was a huge honor for me. Kodansha always featured up and coming pop singers at their party and also all of their comic book (manga) writers and illustrators would be there. I was in heaven! My favorite manga was a series called *Aitsu to Lullabye*, written by Michiharu Kusunoki. There were ultimately 39 volumes in the trade paperback series and I owned and read them all. Since I knew this guy was friends with Nakanishi-sensei, I asked if we could be introduced at the party. These guys were all young and Kusunoki-sensei was only one year older than me. When we met, he couldn't believe that there was an American who was a fan of his series and could read it in Japanese. His comment to me was, "Joe-san, when you read my comics, in the spots where a Japanese would laugh, is that where you laugh too?" The answer was definitely "Yes!" I really enjoyed my conversation with him. The following year, we were invited back to Kodansha's end of year party. I heard, "Joe!" shouted from across the room, and it was Kusunoki-sensei again. I was flattered that he remembered me, but then again, I guess it's hard to forget the only tall non-Japanese person in the whole ballroom.

Nakanishi-sensei and I have remained friends to this day and I try to get together with him whenever I am in Japan.

22 LIFE ON TRAINS

When speaking of trains and social rules, it can get pretty complicated. Much has been written about foreigners and the "empty seat". This refers to the empty seat next to any foreign person riding on a train and I'll add my two cents. If there is another alternative, most of the time a Japanese person will not sit next to a foreigner on a train. My understanding is this is due to the "possible embarrassment" factor. In other words, there is a fear of being spoken to in English in front of the rest of the people on the train and not knowing what to do or say, thus losing face. However, there is also the opposite situation where you get a strange person who understands some English and wants to sit next to you and prod you with seriously personal questions. These are questions they would never dare ask a complete stranger if they were Japanese. One guy was reading a book in English and kept coming to my seat to ask me grammar and pronunciation questions. This all while I'm sitting there reading a comic in Japanese.

Random conversation of two high school girls overheard while walking past them on a local train platform. "Wow, that foreigner is really cute!" "Really? I think his eyes look like a cat!" Okay, I guess I'll take what I can get.

I have a few situations on trains that I will share. One time, I was in a reserved seat on the bullet train, going from Tokyo to Osaka. I had just boarded the train and settled into my seat, when a Japanese guy approached me with the conductor and said that I was sitting in his seat. He was very annoyed that this foreign person could be so foolish as to sit in the wrong seat. I asked him to please show me his ticket. It was all written in Japanese, and yes, this was definitely the seat indicated. However, his ticket was for the next day! I'm ashamed to say that I took great pleasure in pointing this out to him as the conductor escorted him off of the train.

Another time I was travelling to work on a commuter train in Tokyo during rush hour in the first car, when suddenly the train came to a halt. There was a brief delay when the conductor came into our car and said someone had committed suicide by jumping in front of the train. He wanted to know if someone would volunteer to give up their newspaper so that they could cover the body. To my surprise, no one was willing to give up their newspaper and some passengers could be heard complaining that if someone wanted to jump in front of a train, they shouldn't do it during rush hour when they would inconvenience so many other people. I'm not suggesting this is typical Japanese behavior, just something I experienced on that day that was surprising to me. More on experiences with suicide later.

23 DANGER IN TOKYO

In Tokyo during rush hour, there is a train coming every 30 seconds. You may have seen pictures or videos of people cramming onto these trains and then the "pushers" on the platform, wearing white gloves, would gently push the people onto the train so that they could all fit before the doors closed. This could be very hot and uncomfortable, though being six foot tall helped me to be able to breathe! There was one occasion on one of these trains that was packed solid, where a man began to pass out. Actually, he did pass out and when the people around him noticed, they somehow all moved away and he fell to the floor of the train. He was laying on his back and started to vomit. I remember stories of people choking on their own vomit (mainly rock stars) and I leaned down, lifted the guy up and turned him over on his stomach. I then lifted him up and moved him toward the seats along the wall. Initially no one would move out of their seat, but one guy finally did and I was able to have the man sit down. He thanked me as we were just pulling in to the final station where everyone was exiting the train. I waited for the conductor and then exited myself. As I was walking on the platform, I felt a tap on my shoulder. When I turned around, there was a Japanese high school student in his school uniform wordlessly pointing at my shoe and offering me a tissue. I looked down and saw that some of the vomit had gotten on my shoe and this young man had noticed. Somehow that gesture brough tears to my eyes, as I thanked him and he bowed and moved on. At that moment, I realized how we are always being observed and what we do can really make an impression on others and how they perceive us. I hope I made a good impression on that young student and gave him a favorable impression of Americans in general.

One weekend, my Japanese mother-in-law came to stay with us in Tokyo. We had a great visit and when it was time to leave, we went with her to Tokyo Station, so that she could catch the bullet train back to Osaka. While we were walking through the large, crowded station, I saw a young Japanese woman running, screaming "Save me! Save me!". There was a Japanese man chasing her and he grabbed her wrist and caught her about 10 feet in front of me. The woman was still yelling "Save me! Save Me!" but the Japanese people in the crowded station ignored her, not wanting to get involved. Being the clueless foreigner that I am with nothing to lose, I yelled at the guy, "Hey, why don't you leave her alone!" As soon as I said that, a group of Japanese people formed a circle around us, to see what would happen. Some of the Japanese men around the circle, not wanting to be upstaged by the American, began to call out as well, "Yeah, leave her alone!" I'll never forget the look on the guy's face who was holding onto the woman's wrist for dear life. He suddenly looked scared and said "Wait, you don't understand!" Just at that moment, the station conductor showed up and started to talk with the couple. He asked them to come along with him to his office so he could straighten this out and they both meekly followed.

After the incident was over, I realized that I

had no idea what was really happening. I, and eventually all of the others assumed that the man was at fault, because he was chasing the woman and she looked scared and was yelling. However, it could have been possible that she had just run away with all of his money and he had finally tracked her down, and now this clueless American appears out of nowhere and he's suddenly the villain! I never did find out what really happened or who was at fault. However, before it was even over, I noticed my mother-in-law had grabbed her suitcase and was already progressing halfway across the station! There's that "embarrassment factor" at work again.

24 CORPORATE CULTURE

My first client at A.C. Nielsen was the pet food company Purina, which was operated by a joint venture called Purina-Taiyo. The person I replaced at A.C. Nielsen had taken a job at Purina and he was my day to day contact there. We quickly became friends. The head of marketing at Purina was an American guy who did not speak Japanese, though all of his direct reports were Japanese. He used an interpreter. He told me to prepare my slides in English, but to give the presentation in Japanese and he would have his interpreter sit next to him and translate. His logic was that the presentation was really for his people's benefit. The presentation would be given on a bimonthly basis and show how the individual Purina Cat & Dog Food products were selling throughout Japan. The idea was to start with the size of the market and drill down to more detail, telling a story and ending with some action points for the company to take to increase sales. Before I gave the presentation on my own, my boss, whom I'll call T-san was to give the initial presentation to "show me how it's done". He spent a lot of time teaching me different cultural things to be mindful of. Always take your coat off in the lobby and carry it upstairs into the company's offices. The most important person in the meeting always sits furthest from the door. When entering the conference room or someone's office, you always say "Shitsurei Shimasu", which literally means "I'm going to be rude". When entering a conference room, you always wait for someone to direct you to your seat, so you know where they want you to sit. You can always discern who is in charge by way of where they are seated. The way you speak to clients is also different, as you always use very formal Japanese when you are the supplier. Much different when you are just speaking to your friends, for example. When giving any gifts, you always say "Tsumaranai mono desu ga..", which means "this is really nothing special but please accept it". Though he was the one who taught me many valuable lessons, he made a major faux pas during the first meeting.

We were given one hour to conduct the presentation. There was an advertising agency that was to present right when we were finished. As we were coming onto the end of the hour, the ad agency people began gathering in the hallway. This particular agency was famously known for bringing a large group of employees to their meetings, so there were about ten people in the hallway. Regardless of this, my boss proceeded to present for two hours! I could tell by looking at the faces of the recipients that they were not happy, but my boss seemed to be oblivious to this. About thirty minutes after we got back to the office, I received a call from my contact at Purina. His comment was, "next time you come, please make sure you give the presentation and you come by yourself." This was a tough situation for me because I was new in the company and there was no way I could deliver a message like that to my boss. I was already scheduled to present in Japanese at the next meeting in two months' time, so that part was okay. As the date for the next meeting approached, I spent quite a bit of time preparing the presentation and I had to present it to my boss a couple of times for practice. He wanted me to keep practicing late into the evening, but I left at a somewhat reasonable hour and was confident I could pull it off. To this day, I don't like to over practice a presentation, as I feel it removes some of the spontaneity. When I finally gave the presentation, it was a bit strange since I was presenting in Japanese about slides that were titled in English, and the head of marketing had his Japanese interpreter, translating my message back into English. I gave my presentation and respected the time, so I was done in just under one hour. At the conclusion, the room of about ten people burst into applause! It was a great moment for me.

25 ENCOUNTERS WITH SUICIDE

Japan has one of the highest suicide rates of any developed nation, second only to South Korea. I will not try to analyze why so many Japanese people commit suicide, but sometimes it has to do with a mindset that is rooted in their history and culture.

I already talked about my experience with suicide while riding a train, but I also had a few more experiences related to this. One had to do with a Japanese pop star.

Her name was Yukiko Okada and she was only 18 years old when she died. She released her first single two years prior and had played a leading role in a television drama. On April 8, 1986, she tried to kill herself by slashing her wrist and filling her apartment with gas. She was found crying in her closet by a rescue team after neighbors had called about the smell of gas coming from her apartment. Her manager was called and took her to a nearby hospital where she was treated and then released. Her manager then took her to the Sun Music building. While he was discussing with her staff about how to keep this incident out of the media, Yukiko ran up the stairs to the top floor of the building, took off her shoes and jumped. She was killed instantly. There has been much speculation about her motive and it's generally believed it was due to unrequited love for another Japanese actor. This was a huge news story and it led to a number of copycat suicides by young people who wanted to "be with her". These copycat cases were labeled with a new term, "Yukiko Syndrome".

My personal experience was when I worked for the A.C. Nielsen company. I was part of the sales/service division of the company, and a fellow company associate of mine, let's call him "K-san", was working in a separate division. Since I sometimes had to work with that division when my clients were involved, I had met K-san on several occasions. I didn't really know him well, other than the fact that he was married and had a couple of small children. His boss had a bullying type of management style, whereby he would often be yelling at people. Many times I heard him yelling for individuals to come into his office. He had a very gruff manner.

K-san, understandably, did not like his manager and was often at the receiving end of his tirades, causing him to be very stressed. As a result, he approached my manager to see if there were any openings in our department, so that he could transfer out from where he was. These discussions continued, but seemed to be taking an undue amount of time and K-san was growing more and more impatient.

My cubicle was on the eighth floor of a nine-story building. K-san's cubicle was on a lower floor. One day, I arrived at the office early and noticed K-san standing near the window on our floor by the printer, looking out. I said good morning to him. He greeted me and then left the floor. After about ten minutes, one of the administrative assistants on my team had just arrived and came running onto the eighth floor yelling "K-san just killed himself!". I couldn't believe it, as I had just seen him ten minutes prior. After greeting me, he must have walked up the stairs to the ninth floor and jumped out of the window. It seems that he was trying to make a statement by landing right at the building entrance right when employees would be arriving to work. He had at least a one hour commute to the office, so he came all the way into Tokyo to jump out of the building where he worked. We were all in shock. Even creepier were the phones, usually always ringing but now silent, except for mine. I answered it. It was one of my clients who used to work with me at A.C. Nielsen and was a personal friend of K-san. I told him about K-san's suicide and I was shocked when he commented that he wasn't even surprised about his death. He must have been much more knowledgeable about K-san's situation than I was.

The next morning, I noticed a small group of managers walking around the office near the eighth floor window. K-san's young widow was with them. It seems that they were showing her K-san's actions in the last minutes of his life. I was further shocked when his widow approached me and handed me a small gift. She handed out gifts to everyone on our team and apologized for the trouble her husband had caused the company. The gift was a small hand towel, boxed and wrapped. I couldn't imagine what this poor woman with two young children at home must have been feeling that day. K-san's suicide really affected me. It was sad he felt his only way out was to kill himself. It never occurred to him to try to go work for a competitor or to try and find a job outside of the company. I think the feeling that the Japanese company was like an extended family where you stayed for life, may have been a factor in his thinking. Even though it was a non-Japanese company, the culture was very Japanese with all Japanese employees other than myself and the company president.

Another encounter with suicide was with my previous company, Shimaden; though it happened after I had moved on. I don't have all of the details other than the person who killed himself was known to me and was really a nice guy. He was quite a bit older than I was. The building was only four stories tall and it seems he climbed to the roof of the building and threatened to jump, while a number of company employees looked on. Eventually he did jump, but only managed to break his leg. He was taken to the hospital and suffered from quite a bit of embarrassment over the episode.

Irony of ironies, about one year after this incident, he was admitted to the hospital for heart surgery and unexpectedly died during the procedure. It was so sad that when he actually wanted to live, he died.

26 RESTAURANTS: A OR B SET?

Just to be clear, I am not a food person or a "foodie". I have always been thin and like to say that I "eat to live" and not "live to eat"! Therefore, my food stories are not so much about the magnificent food choices that are available in Japan, as they are about rules around what can be ordered in restaurants and whether or not those rules can be bent (hint: most of the time they cannot).

We had a Denny's restaurant that was about 20 minutes away from our house in Sakado, by car. In the US, the Denny's chain had something called a "Denny's Combo" which consisted of a hamburger and a small salad. In Japan, the Denny's menu was much different than the one in the US. There were many

Japanese style dishes along with individual odd choices such as potato salad, or buttered corn. In order to work at a food restaurant in Japan, it was necessary for the servers to go through an extensive training. This was not just at Denny's but everywhere. For example, they were all required to memorize the contents of the menu and then trained to set the glasses, dishes, etc. down in front of the customer without making any noise. This is in direct contrast with the US where servers at chain style restaurants just seem to slam the coffee cups or silverware down in front of you. Or throw the dishes into the tray or bin when cleaning the table with much clatter. In Japan, it's a much more civilized experience. The only downside is that there are still smoking sections in most restaurants, so they can tend to be quite smokey, where the western world has pretty much banned smoking indoors in restaurants.

I would always look forward to our visits to Denny's, as it reminded me of home, though the menu was quite different. There was one thing on the menu that was the same, however. There was a Denny's combo, which featured a hamburger. I would always look forward to going to Denny's for this very reason. However, nine times out of ten, I would order the Denny's combo and the server would make an apologetic expression before saying, "I'm sorry, we are all out of bread." At that point, I would have to order something else, but my mood would be deflated. Now, you think I would have learned over time that this would happen more often than not, as I was in Japan after all. However, I would naively continue to repeat this time and time again. Oh well.

Whenever we would go out to lunch in Japan, regardless of the restaurant, there was typically a lunch menu that had a selection of the "A Set" or "B Set". These were daily lunch features that were priced reasonably and most people would choose one or the other to avoid having to make any major decisions at lunch. Years later, when my Japanese in-laws came to visit us in the US for the first time and we took them out to lunch, it was at a chain such as TGIF or Appleby's, etc. They did not speak any English and when the lunch menu came, it contained about 8-10 pages. They were amazed at all of the choices and I was put in the position of having to translate 10 pages of food choices! In that sense, the Japanese system was much easier. In addition, outside every Japanese restaurant they have plastic replicas of the food dishes that are served inside. Therefore, even if you don't speak Japanese, you could have the server follow you outside the restaurant where you could point to what you wanted to eat.

The downside of the A and B sets was that there were no substitutions, and this could drive you a bit crazy, especially if you're not the type of person who orders things "off the rack" or "off the shelf". For example, the meal would tend to come with a soft drink. However, if you wanted to order a cup of coffee or tea in place of the soft drink, you were told that you can order that separately at a separate price, but you would have to have the soft drink whether you wanted it or not, because it was included in the set. This could get a little crazy; once at McDonalds a friend of mine wanted to have barbecue sauce with the chicken tenders. He was told that barbeque sauce was only for chicken nuggets, and was refused.

The best example of this was when my wife and I decided to go to an Italian restaurant near Haneda airport in Tokyo for dinner. Italian food is one of my favorites and I was pleasantly surprised at all of the choices on the menu. I saw that they had spaghetti and meatballs, as well as mostaccioli (penne pasta). Great! I could almost taste the sauce already. When the server came to our table, I said I would like to have the mostaccioli and meatballs. She looked at me with a very sorrowful and concerned expression on her face. "I'm sorry sir, but mostaccioli does not come with meatballs." Hmm. "Well, you have spaghetti and meatballs, correct?" Now her face brightened up. "Oh yes! Would you like to have the spaghetti and meatballs?" "Um, no thank-you. How about if you take the meatballs off of the spaghetti plate and you put them onto my mostaccioli plate?" Her expression turned apologetic again and she made a sound of sucking in air, which is a way of saying that will not be possible and she was not sure how to answer. However, to her credit, she said "I will have to go and consult with the chef." Great! I thought, here we go, we're really getting somewhere now. After about five minutes the server returned with the chef in tow. The chef looked at me, bowed and said, "I'm sorry sir, the mostaciolli does not come with meatballs, but if you want us to add meatballs to the mostaciolli, we will have to charge you separately. It will be an additional 100 yen." Finally, a decision maker! Though now 100 yen is close to US $1.00, back then it was only about fifty cents. I said "Yes! That would be great!" It seems the misunderstanding in this case was they thought I wanted to receive the meatballs at no charge, as if they were part of the meal, when I just wanted to eat meatballs and had no issue paying extra for them. Both sides breathed a sigh of relief that this impasse had been resolved (not to mention my wife, who was dying of embarrassment! Definitely not the first time.) Maybe this was part of the reason we were denied apartments!

In Japan, there is a donut chain called Mr. Donuts. It's similar to the US chain called Dunkin' Donuts, but the donuts at Mr. Donuts are less sweet. The Japanese palate does not like things overly sweet as we do in America, so any type of candy bar, cakes, etc. are always made with less sugar and are quite good. This might be more of a language issue, than a food story, but I thought it was pretty funny. On my way home from work one day, I decided to stop at Mr. Donuts to get some of my favorite double chocolate donuts to bring home. Upon entering the shop, I noticed there were only four double chocolate donuts left in the case. When it was my turn, I said "please give me all of your double chocolate donuts, to go." The clerk behind the counter, looking at me with a panicked expression said, "ALL of them?!" I replied, "Well, how about just four of them?" He breathed a sigh of relief. "Oh, thanks!" (again, there were only four double chocolate donuts). Another crisis averted.

Another food situation, this time involving borrowed English words (gairaigo), had to do with Domino's Pizza. The Domino's Pizza chain had come to our area of Tokyo and they had a pizza delivery business. I thought, that's fantastic! Now we can order American style pizza from the comfort of our own home. I took a look at the menu, and having pretty boring food tastes, I decided to order a cheese pizza. Nothing fancy for me! I picked up the phone and dialed the number.

"Domino's Pizza, how can we help you?"
"I would like to order a cheese pizza."
"Um, they all come with cheese, sir."

I could see here that I was missing something, as I obviously understood pizzas all have cheese. After much back and forth about pizza ingredients, I finally understood the issue. It turns out that I was to use the borrowed English word "plain" when ordering a pizza that only contained cheese. The next time I ordered a cheese pizza, I was a complete success.

"I would like to order a plain pizza."
"Great! Thanks for your order, will that be all?"

Live and learn! Sometimes understanding how borrowed English words are incorporated into the Japanese language was more difficult than learning the Japanese language in general. Some examples:

Ice:	Ice Cream
Pan:	Bread (borrowed from Spanish)
Depaato:	Department Store
Rimokon:	TV Remote Control
Waishatsu:	Dress Shirt (White Shirts)
Baiku:	Motorcycle (Bike)
Zubon:	Pants (borrowed from French)
Pantsu:	Underwear (Pants)

One interesting scenario happened when some American clients of mine visited Japan and were staying in a hotel in Tokyo. One evening, they decided to have some drinks in their room and they called room service for some ice. They were speaking in English, of course, but in Japanese, the word "ice" means "ice cream", so room service brought them ice cream. They realized they had not made themselves clear, so they called room service and tried again. Ten minutes later, another round of ice cream was dutifully delivered! They never did resolve the issue and when they relayed this story to me the next day, I understood immediately what had happened and explained it to them. Ah, the magic of language!

Between the train station and my office at Shimaden, there was a small sandwich shop. The sandwiches seemed to model those from the UK, as they had things like tuna fish and cucumber, strawberries and cream, etc. I went into the shop one day and noticed they had peanut butter sandwiches and separately they had jam sandwiches. Growing up in the US, I had eaten many peanut butter and jelly sandwiches over the years, so I grew a bit nostalgic. I asked the clerk behind the counter if I could have a peanut butter and jam sandwich. He looked at me as if I had just lost my mind. "We have peanut butter sandwiches and we have jam sandwiches, sir." I said, "yes, I can see that. But can you please put peanut butter on one slice of bread, jam on the other and combine them into one sandwich please?" He made a face and said, "How could you eat that?" I was wondering how anyone could eat strawberries and cream in a sandwich, but such are differing cultures! In the end, he made it and it was delicious. Sadly, that's the last time I went there, since it really wasn't worth the effort to try again.

27 THE MAGIC OF COMPANY TRIPS

My first exposure to the company trip was when I was still living in the city of Numata where things were very traditional. In this case, it wasn't actually a company, but the government education office of which I was a member. Traditionally, Japanese companies are viewed very much as a family, so the company trip is an annual event that is understood to be required. The strange part to me, was that no spouses were invited along for the trip. I was single, so it didn't really affect me in that way, but I saw it was understood and accepted by the spouses of the company employees that they were not invited.

The trip typically involved traveling to a

Japanese Inn (Ryokan) for one or two nights. Upon arrival, by chartered bus in most cases, the employees are assigned to tatami matted rooms. Everyone then changes into yukata, which are thin cotton Kimono type robes with a separate sash tie. You will often see these made available in any Japanese hotel. These are worn around the Inn by the guests and also used to sleep in. For me, the ones provided by any Japanese hotel or Inn were always too short. Because of this, I decided to do some prior preparation. A number of weeks before the trip, I visited a local kimono shop with a friend of mine. She was there to have a proper kimono made for a wedding she was attending. I tagged along and asked if they could make a custom yukata for me, so that I would have one that fit me properly on the trip. They were happy to do so. They took the required measurements and within a week or so, the yukata was completed and ready to take along on the trip.

These company trips were quite the experience. Before dinner, people make their way to the communal baths. These can also be hot springs, depending on the location. Men and women have separate areas, but the men all bathe together and so do the women. The baths are large pools of very hot water. There is a row of spigots and plastic stools along the wall, usually with a small mirror in front of each. There each person lathers up and washes their bodies before descending into the hot bath. There is also shampoo/conditioner to wash your hair. Typically, each person is just provided with a small washcloth which they can also take into the bath for some modesty. The hot water takes some getting used to but it's a good time to relax and converse.

Once the bath is concluded, everyone dries off, gets back into their yukata and heads for the dining area. This is typically a large tatami matted room with low tables and everyone sits on the floor to dine on a pre-selected meal which is served in courses. Typically, beer or juice is also served with the meal.

Once the meal is complete, there is usually some entertainment, such as Japanese traditional dancers or a singer. While this is happening, the liquor (traditional sake and beer) begins to flow. It is customary for each person to pour drinks for others (you never fill your own cup) and everyone takes turns filling the cup of the company president and senior members. The cups you are pouring into are sometimes already full, but you pour anyway to honor the tradition. The senior members can't possibly drink all that is poured and you sometimes see cups emptied into nearby plants, etc. In Japan there is something called 'tatemae" (behavior and opinions one displays in public) and "honne" (true feelings). Once people start to drink, their true feelings and thoughts (honne) start to come out. Traditionally, what is said while drinking is "forgotten" the next day.

At this time, some people will break off to play a game such as mahjong, or they will queue up to sing karaoke, etc.

On the company trip with the government education office, most of the members of our office were older men and very traditional in their behavior. However, when I worked for the Shimaden company, the makeup of our office consisted of people of all ages, both male and female, so there were quite a few people my own age. Because of this, I had a bit of a rude awakening at the Shimaden company outing. When it was time for people to change into their yukata for dinner, I once again had brought my custom made one that fit me. However, since this company was based in Tokyo and had a number of younger employees, they were a bit more lax in their tradition. I walked into the dining room dressed in yukata, and all the others my age were lounging around in their jeans and street clothes! Once again, I was more Japanese than the Japanese people, to my embarrassment. I realized that the "traditions" I had learned in the country didn't always apply with the city crowd.

28 SAYING GOODBYE

After living in Japan for eight years, it was finally time to move back to the US. For me, it was moving back, but for my wife and one year old son, it would be their first experience living in another country. I liked to joke that "most people come back from Japan with a t-shirt, but I came back with a wife and son!"

The previous year I had taken a group of Japanese clients of the A.C. Nielsen Company, along with my boss on a company tour of the US, where we visited Chicago, New York and Washington DC. I had arranged for hotels and limousines in each city, as well as serving as the interpreter for the group. As part of the trip, we visited Northbrook, Illinois, where A.C. Nielsen had their global headquarters. As part of that trip, I learned that the company had recently started a group to sell market research data across 25+ countries (now 100) and they could use someone with knowledge of Japanese and how local countries produced information. It seemed perfect for me and now I had been offered a position in Northbrook. Coincidentally, I had grown up and lived my whole life in a town only forty minutes away from there. This prompted my father to say, "you mean to tell me you had to move all the way to Japan to take a job 40 minutes away from here?" It sounds funny, but it was really true. There is no way I would have been offered that global role without the cultural and language experience I received by living in Japan all of those years.

As of this writing, we are still living in the US, but we have been back to visit Japan once per year since. I realized long ago that by loving two countries so much, we would always be missing someone in Japan by living in the US and vice versa. It's so much easier now with social media, Facetime, Skype, etc., to keep in touch with people across the world. Back when I lived in Japan, we only had letters (snail mail) and phone calls that would cost over $2.00 per minute from a landline. The longest I had been away from the US without visiting was two years. When I came back to visit after two years of being away, it was major reverse culture shock for me, as everything was frozen in time in my memory. These days, people are in touch electronically in real time and it is much easier. There are also many more non-Japanese people who can speak Japanese fluently and it is not as much of a novelty as it was then. Even with all of the obstacles I faced without the internet, etc., I would not trade my experiences in Japan for anything.

ABOUT THE AUTHOR

Joe Palermo grew up in Addison, Illinois. Upon graduation from the University of Illinois at Chicago, he moved to Japan to accept a position with the Japanese government as a Mombusho English Fellow (MEF). He spent 3 years working for Shimaden, a Japanese manufacturer of industrial temperature controllers and then joined the Nielsen company (formerly A.C. Nielsen) locally in Japan. His career at Nielsen spanned 25 years in various corporate roles focused on global market research, which brought him back to the US. He worked for 6 years in a global capacity for Information Resources, Inc (IRI) where he established several global services. He is now semi-retired and lives with his wife in the suburbs of Chicago.

Printed in Great Britain
by Amazon